Hope Rising

HOPE RISES LIKE A PHOENIX FROM THE ASHES OF SHATTERED DREAMS

—

S. A. SACHS

Ancient legends describe the fiery death of the magical bird, the Phoenix, and its stunning rebirth, as it rises, wings unfurling, from the ashes, to begin a new life.

Anti-apartheid lawyer Albie Sachs was tortured, imprisoned, and lost an arm and the sight of one eye when a bomb set by South African Security Forces blew up under his car. Afterward, Sachs did not seek revenge, but instead sought what he calls "soft vengeance, the triumph of your life, of your ideas, of your goals."

Hope Rising

A MUSING

To help you feel better about life,
love and the future of humankind.

by
Kathy Eldon

and
her Noisy Spirits

Waterside Productions

Printed in the United States of America

First Printing, 2021

ISBN-13: 978-1-951805-45-6 print edition
ISBN-13: 978-1-951805-46-3 ebook edition

Waterside Productions
2055 Oxford Ave
Cardiff, CA 92007
www.waterside.com

Managing Editor: Alicia Dougherty

Editor: Nicole Melillo

Illustrations: Kathy Eldon

Art Direction/Design: Kyle Hollingsworth/www.kyle-creative.com

Cover: Kyle Hollingsworth & Nicole Melillo

This book is dedicated to the wondrous children
of our planet, especially Jack, Daniel and Arabella Turteltaub,
Mac, Jimmy and Mila Bedner, and Indra and Bodhi Bedner.

Hope Rising

A MUSING

1 CORONA BLUES AND SOME GOOD NEWS   **1**

Hope in the Air   2
Staycation   4
Safety Zone   6
Bounce   8
Unmasking Good   10
Cocooned   14

2 LOVE BEFORE, DURING AND   **16**
AFTER A PANDEMIC

Tinder/Tender   18
In the Mood   20
Play Date   25
Heart. Cracked. Open.   28
Love Lost, Love Found, Sort of   32
Journey of the Souls   36
How Do I Love You?   38

3 BECOMING ME   **42**

Grace   44
I Am Woman   46
Red Lady   48
A Box Called Me   50
Playing Hooky   54
Free at Last   59
If Only   60

4 TINKERING WITH LIFE, TOYING WITH DEATH   **62**

Playing with DNA   66
Where Do We Go When We Die?   70
Blink   72
Phantom Limb   74
Finding Wings to Fly   76
Noisy Spirits   78

5 A BETTER TOMORROW   **82**

Get in the Way   84
For One and For All   86
Purple Heart   88
A Sweet Solution   90
This is Your Mother Speaking   96
A New Creation   100

HOPE RISING: A FINAL MUSING   **103**

AFTERWORD BY SOME OF MY NOISY SPIRITS   **104**

A Musing

Five months into the COVID-19 shutdown, strange words flowing through my mind awakened me in the middle of the night. Sleepy and annoyed, I whispered them into my phone so my husband wouldn't wake up. The next morning, I was startled to read the opening lines of my first-ever poem, "Imagine a Nation."

Over the next few weeks, I recorded bits of spoken word poetry that continued to pour through me. Given that I have never written poems before, I attributed the creative outpouring to the noisy spirits who seem to hover around me, full of advice and ideas, if I am ever quiet enough to listen. I suspected that one of my muses was a cool rapper cut down in mid verse, or a frustrated poet trapped in purgatory, who chose me to transmit messages to people of the 21st century, also confined to an unfamiliar space between the life we knew, and the unknown existence that lies ahead.

Although I was aware of the presence of Noisy Spirits before the death of my son, Dan, since then, I have felt him to be the ringleader of a motley crew of dearly departed souls who have convinced me that we can communicate with those who are no longer physically present - and that they have important things to tell us. Top of their list is a stern reminder that if we don't connect with one another to save our endangered planet, we are doomed as a species. If we hear what they are saying, heed the words of scientists and each do our bit, our children's children's children can not only survive, but even thrive.

This unlikely collection also includes snippets from my memoir, *In the Heart of Life,* and guided journals, written by my daughter Amy and me, about love, loss and finding new purpose in our lives. In *Hope Rising*, I have also shared wise, often witty inspiration from my mentors, teachers and guides, both invisible and visible.

I hope my musings inspire you to open yourself to use the blank pages in the book to open yourself to Noisy Spirits who may have something important (or very silly) to share with you - and the world.

With love,

Kathy Eldon

CHAPTER 1

Corona Blues and Some Good News

On March 9th, 2020, our world shut down. Always a social person, my schedule filled with back-to-back meetings and a continuous flow of visitors, friends and random people off the beach, I found the enforced isolation to be soul-numbing. As the world imploded with multiple challenges, including a rising Covid death toll and protests around social justice and smoke swirling from fires ignited as a result of climate change, paralysis took over. Don't even get me started about economic hardships faced by much of the world's population, as well as the anxieties and fears about the challenges we face as individuals and as members of a global community.

It seems that the shutdown brought us some unexpected benefits - like the realization of how little we actually require, as opposed to desire, as well as more time for family dinners and Zoom connections with friends, old and new, around the world. Most surprising for me, the unaccustomed peace and extra sleep allowed space for these rhyming words that have come, unbidden, through me. By listening to the thoughts expressed in the poems, I have been able to come out of hiding, move beyond my fears and imagine a brighter future, one filled with hope and determination, a brand new creation for myself - our nation - and for our world.

Hope in the Air

So what's the best solution to the Pandemic?
Vaccinate, inoculate us all with bleach?
Here's another idea ...

Overnight we lost our purpose,
all that kept us all from feeling worthless.
Shut down, deprived of sky,
locked away alone together,
wondering when, why or even whether
our lives would ever get better.
With nowhere to go, no one to see,
with nothing much to acquire
we saw how little we actually require.

As we slid into despair,
hope suddenly appeared in the air.
John Krasinski's "good news" delighted
with visions of a world united.
It was a novel infection that eluded detection,
promising herd immunity from our lack of community.

With that loving cure revealed
we almost felt healed.
But time passes and the time passed

and now we're out together unmasked,
essential existential questions unasked.

Amazon and the market booming,
evictions, bankruptcies and a recession looming.
Fear. Protest. Racial oppression.
Pandemic raging. Democracy fraying.
The global climate is definitely changing.

So what now?
Vaccinate, inoculate,
inject us all with bleach?
No. We need to remind us
to cure ourselves with kindness
If we want to heal the painful breach.

Masking differences,
social distance without resistar
Seek a solution, not dissolutior
Learn to share and to care.
Unity in community.
Bring it on. With impunity.

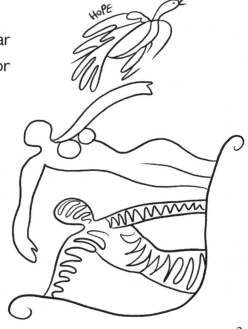

Staycation

As the shutdown continued, I decided to use my fears as stepping stones and liberate myself from anxiety and self-doubt. But during uncertain times, sometimes all I want is for everything to go back to normal.

I always longed for a new lease on life,
time off for good behavior,
a chance to savor the flavor of slow-cooked meals,
instead of those delivered on wheels.
Idle hours to play a board game
without the slightest hint of shame.
I ached to sleep in till eleven
and trundle off to bed at seven.

When Covid hit and we were shut away,
it was a joy at first, until we had to stay
in the house day after day after day.
When my staycation
stopped being a fun vacation,
I yearned to venture beyond my door,
but being out soon became a bore
as masked breathing turned into a chore.

Now I choose to stay at home
because it's no fun to roam.

4

Bored and frustrated,
I yearn to be unregulated,
free to fly to far-away places
or just mingle in crowded spaces.

I'm nostalgic for germs that cause colds and sneezes
wafting over gentle breezes.
Allow me to sit by an unmasked stranger
without feeling a hint of danger.
Let me blast out a song in an amateur choir
or share s'mores around a cozy camp fire.
Please release me from this new lease on life
and let me return to the swirl and the strife.

Safety Zone

In the past months, many of us have had emotional ups and downs as we have faced situations out of our control. I have learned that it is okay to feel hurt, upset, betrayed, even depressed or anxious about what's happening in the world around me. What is not okay is to let my anger or frustration devour me, or leave me feeling dejected, powerless, devoid of energy and hope. Channeling my frustration into writing helped me get back up when I was feeling down, and think about how I could find solutions to the challenges we face, like getting sunburned during a pandemic.

Bake, braise, grill or fry,

So how do you want to die?

Lying on a bed of sand, Margarita in hand,

rare, medium or well done after a day in the searing sun.

Sounds like heaps of fun

though every kid over seven

knows it speeds your trip to heaven.

Melanoma, freckles or a burn

when will we ever learn

that broiling bodies is not cool?

With Covid there is another rule.

As we go to the beach, we must teach

ourselves to social distance without resistance.

If you want to get up close and personal
you must be diligent and merciful.
Wear a mask. Though you may gasp
it will create a protective zone
from the nasty hole in the ozone.
Cheating corona, defeating melanoma,
so you can die later of sarcoma.

Bounce

During times of heightened stress, we must ask for the help we need to find positive solutions to the problems we face. We must take control of our lives and not stay in the pain. We cannot always change what is happening to us, but we can change our way of handling it. In other words, get up, put on pants with a zipper and cut your hair, dammit.

I'm down today, afraid and sad,
hurting inside, feeling bad.
I thought that I would soon be well,
but I don't know how to get out of this living hell.
Depressed by the gloom that suffocates me,
confined, constricted, restricted and worse
I have to get rid of what feels like a curse.

I will rise from my bed and open the door,
I will banish the night with luminous light
I will leave this room filled with yesterday's sorrow
and focus on creating a better tomorrow.

I will find peace and release in simple things,
the joy that a friend or a flower brings.
I will trade my sweatpants for those with a zipper
and attack my hair with an Amazon clipper.
Gloom at bay I will Zoom my friends
and say that I will live for another day.
Positive and hopeful I will remain
until tomorrow when I will start this all over again.

Unmasking Good

In old pre-Covid days, I never heard anybody ask,
"Please, may I wear a mask?"
Except, of course on Halloween
when girls wore them to look like a queen
and kids donned them trying to be
Spiderman, Supergirl or the notorious RBG.

There are masks of another kind,
those we hide ourselves behind,
hoping no one will pull them off and say,
"And just who, my friend, are you today?"

I am discussing masks
defined as those designed
to protect you if someone sick sneezes,
and the sneeze travels over breezes
and lands on you and you get sick too.
Annoying masks that when you speak,
make muffled mumbles sound like Greek.

Masks that get glasses smoggy,
paper ones soggy,
and face shields foggy.
On the other hand, three-ply cotton covers

will block dangerous particulates,

though they suck if you wish to be articulate,

without having to gesticulate.

Swashbuckling bandanas are ineffective.

In fact, according to a recent scientific directive,

when you cough they are downright defective.

Fortunately we can now be mask-selective,

unlike in the early days of Covid,

when, it should be noted

masks were limited online.

But now the lure of haute couture

means you can choose from many refined designs.

So, select your mask with care and wear it with a smile.

You'll be glad you went that extra mile,

for if your eyes really crinkle above your hidden dimple,

though your face may feel that it's under a shroud,

you'll feel proud when the grin buried within,

coupled with an elbow bump,

will take you out of your slump and over the hump

as you melt the heart of the grumpiest old grump.

Your Turn

These pages are for your thoughts and ideas. Here are a couple of questions to get you started.

Imagine a descendent is reading this 50 years from now. How would you describe your life before, during and after the pandemic?

Before - was ready for change. Needed it. felt like I would die w/out it. Needed to be jolted to make better decision

During - started to make those choice. Quit smoking. Drank less. Moved out of the city. Eating better. Exercising more. Having adventures. Tapping into passions,

... and then it all starts to feel the same...

Cocooned

I make reference to the "Bubble Boy," David Vetter, born in 1971 with a severe auto-immune illness that confined him to a plastic bubble until he died at the age of 12.

He doesn't look up when I walk by.
Even if I say hi.
He stares straight ahead,
eyes dead.

I want to scream,
stop peering at a screen
and live your life first hand.
But it is a useless demand,
for he is forced to exist in a bubble
like the boy I read about
whose story made me cry
because he would die
if he ever left the tiny place
that was his only safe space.

My heart goes out to kids
who yearn to play
away from fathers and mothers,
their sisters and their brothers,

who too are desperate
to visit a zoo,
swim in a pool, or go to school.

Instead of being free to roam,
they have to stay home.
Bubble-wrapped, safety-capped,
insured, preserved, insulated
and cocooned from anything
that might cause them harm.
As time goes by they sigh,
waiting for a chance to break out and fly.

Written by Arabella, age 5 1/2

CHAPTER 2

Love before, during and after a Pandemic

As we discovered during the coronavirus shutdown, the need to be loved, nurtured and appreciated is a challenging premise during a pandemic. Some of us long for romance, while others want a real companion to give us more than a virtual hug. Many yearn for the rebirth of an old relationship or need guidance to help separate from a longtime companion. We want quality time with our children, the little ones who Zoom-bomb our meetings, and the bigger ones, phones in hand, who are aching for true connection with their friends. We want to nurture far-away parents, and find new ways to be good friends and family members in a socially-distanced world.

Whether before, during or after the pandemic, we all want more love in our lives, but often we don't know where to find it. We don't realize that to be loved, we must learn to love. To receive love, we must give it, not only to others, but to ourselves. We don't have to rely on anyone else, for inside each one of us is an infinite source of loving energy. We just have to open the tap and let it flow.

It is then that we discover love is everywhere. Love is in the infinite mysteries of nature and the miracle of simply being alive. Love is in an unexpected email from a faraway friend, in momentary encounters with a masked stranger, whose eyes connect with ours. We can give and receive love in a gesture, a silent prayer, meditation, a gift of appreciation, or in an unexpected phone call. Give love away and you'll find it pouring back.

Tinder/Tender

The absolutely frustrating pursuit of a mate in the time of social media

During a time of Tinder
whatever happened to being tender?
As in the lingering touch of a finger,
stroking a cheek or an arm,
a not-so-innocent gesture
meant to charm or disarm,
not alarm, like a mean screen swipe.

Left/right, right/left,
now quickly assess.
Is she/he more or is he/she less?
Your decision is based on a guess.
He/she is an okay height,
But you say she/he's just not right.
I'd be inclined to sit tight,
better flight than fight

Left/right, right/left.
I'm getting stressed, really distressed
by this depressing quest.
Is there another way you could suggest?
You say flirt in a park, a gallery or bar?
Do people even do that anymore?

Feels like a bore. A chore. A total snore.
Left/right, right/left,
It's the big night.
A movie and out for a bite.
Mmm ... is eye contact indicated?
Or is that concept outdated?
Should you hold his/her chair?
Gently brush back her/his hair?
Will it faze you if the other person pays?
Or was that just a feminist phase?

Later at his/her place,
do you invade her/his space
and use his/her toothpaste?
then hug or snuggle, cuddle or spoon?
Lie on the sofa and gaze at the moon?
Do you try to hook up?
Or just sit, iPhones in hand,
binging Netflix series on demand.
OMG the next day
after coffee and toast
it could be over - cancel or ghost.
He/she/they could go totally silent
or obnoxiously boast.

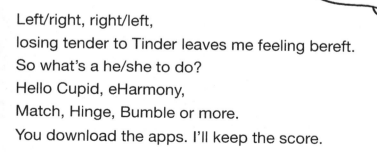

Left/right, right/left,
losing tender to Tinder leaves me feeling bereft.
So what's a he/she to do?
Hello Cupid, eHarmony,
Match, Hinge, Bumble or more.
You download the apps. I'll keep the score.

In the Mood

Before you decide to procreate, take a moment.

I lost me when we became three.
Before, when we were just two,
me and he, I was free to be ...
well, for starters, alone when I pee.
Then we added another and soon a baby brother
which meant quiet time was no longer mine.

Having company 24/7 made being alone feel like heaven.
Waking up in the night,
making sure the kids were alright
left me hazy, lazy and let's face it,
more than a little crazy.

There were other problems too.
When I was a new mother
I sometimes tried to hide from my partner, my lover,
I hated to be rude, but rarely was I in the mood,
and besides, when we started to snuggle,
I was turned off by his scratchy stubble.

Being a married couple has joys we know,
but when your nuclear family starts to grow

some of the glow is bound to go.

So slow down and enjoy each other

before you decide to create another.

Make love all night, then delight

in taking a drive without *Frozen*

playing for the five-hundredth time.

Practice yoga without a baby on your back

or with your teen offering annoying feedback.

Sleep in as long as you like or take a hike without a crying tyke.

Extend your courtship and stabilize your relationship

before you add another, lose your grip and tip the ship.

But if you have left it too late, do not despair.

If you take enough antidepressants

you can survive your adolescents.
With luck they'll leave home
and you'll find yourselves alone
staring at each other across the table
daydreaming about the way it used to be,
when the house was full and the refrigerator empty.
No food, thanks to your insatiably hungry brood.

Hey, with no distractions from the multitude
a renewed attraction may put you in the mood —
so turn out the lights and prepare to delight
in the pleasures ahead in the quiet of night.
Like sleep. Uninterrupted and deep.
Sigh…

How are your relationships?

With yourself ... your family ... your partner?

Feeling stuck. Depressed. Too much change at once. Makes me depressed I guess. Have anxiety. Not want to move. I wish he cared enough to ask me. Or hold me. Or make love to me.

If there is room for improvement, what will you do about it?

I can't do anything. If I show him I want him, he comes up w/ an excuse to pull away.
I guess I'll just be patient
And write songs

Play Date

Relationships are like most ships. They can keel over if we aren't careful.

Can we just stay in bed and play today?
When we're hungry we'll run down the street
for a quick drink and a bite to eat.
Then we'll hurry back, crawl under the sheets,
tell Alexa to turn the volume down low
while we make love, above and below,
and later bask in the afterglow.

Promise me that we'll always agree
to be romantic and carefree
Say that you'll never outgrow me
and I'll do the same.
We'll never blame each other
but cherish one another,
give and forgive,
as long as we both shall live.

Three months later,

Darling, could you hand me the remote?
What? You won't change the channel until we vote?
That makes me angry and out of sorts,
sick to death of your constant sports.
I want to watch the Hallmark channel,
Anderson Cooper and a CNN panel.
I will scream if we have to see your wretched team
score another goal at the Super Bowl.
You are totally out of control!

You on the other hand
can hardly moan about me.
You're always on the phone
with that confidential tone
that feels to me like a no go zone.
You drone on about how I should reveal what I feel.
Well, I would if we could have a conversation
about sports, movies or the state of the nation.

Hey, let's stop all this talk
and go for a walk around the block.
Take stock and remember the promises
we made to one another
to love and cherish each other.

Sorry, if I sound rude,
but I am really not in the mood.
The laundry needs folding,
the dishwasher loading.
A Zoom call looms,
my boss is on hold
and if truth be told,
there's no freaking way
I can get away and play.
You will have to try for another day.

Heart. Cracked. Open.

We never think it will happen to us. When we fall in love we imagine there may be rocky stretches but we don't plan on the really hard times, when the pain of love gone wrong throws us off balance, threatens our self-esteem and destroys our peace of mind. As we grapple through the dark tunnel of despair, we often ask ourselves, why, if we once loved each other so deeply, why must we hurt one another so much? How can we find a loving way through the darkness?

Never be reckless with someone else's heart,

he said, just before we parted,

or rather he departed,

leaving me in uncharted waters

without a rudder, or even a boat

to cruise around the moat

that encircled the castle

that guarded his heart.

Although I splashed and flailed,

I failed to scale the stone walls

guarding the inner halls

where he stayed,

ready to prey on another like me.

Someone eager to be loved like no other

until there was another.

Heart. Cracked. Open. Totally broken,

I cried until something inside me died.

So when he called to say hey, how are you doing?

I replied. You are dead to me.

Suddenly I felt free, oblivious to his plea

that the latest other was no more. Out the door.

Later I found her floating in the moat

so I took her home, dried her tears

and soothed her fears.

Together we clinked glasses,

cheers we said, downing our beers.

Never
be reckless with
Someone else's heart.

I need to hear loving words

Here are the words I'd like to hear ...

Thank you for taking care of us.
I love you.
You're amazing.
You do so much
I want you
I need you

I will say more loving words

Here are the words I'd like to say ...

I'm so proud of you
You're amazing

Love Lost, Love Found, Sort of

For those of you who have memories of an old love rattling
around in your head and heart ... and really, who doesn't?

Did you ever try to relocate a former amour
who refuses to vacate your mind,
even though you meant to leave them behind?
Is there a box tucked under your bed
filled with letters frequently read,
loving words stuck in your head,
though the one who wrote them to you
is to you, or so you said, definitely dead.
Have you ever been to a class reunion
seeking reunion with an old heart throb,
one you cannot seem to release
even though, if one of you doesn't let go,
you will never be at peace.

Did you ever want to see,
or better still be with one you once loved but lost?
Spend a day, say, as a way to allay feelings
that can still have you reeling,
though best not to spend the night
if you don't want to trigger fight or flight,
that will only complicate your plight.

Do you feel aching, burning, yearning,
or a piercing pain that leaves you
pondering, wondering, worrying
about how, when or whether
you two will ever be together -
for a moment or forever?

Here is what you should do.
Replace the partner of your illusion
with a new one sans delusion
firmly planted in the here and now.
No more scheming or dreaming
about a fuzzy future when, if or how.

With your new love
be careful not to share unbidden your ex's name,
for you may reveal hidden feelings
best kept concealed about your former flame.
Remember, incendiary sparks once set alight,
may ignite pale embers, which fanned till bright,
could implode and explode into a wild wildfire
that if not quickly restrained will be impossible to contain.

So stay in the present.
Consider your partner a gift
and avoid doing anything stupid
that could create a rift.
Celebrate life, avoid strife
and delight in the dazzling light
that surrounds this beloved other.
Another one, who one day, I pray
will not join the ranks of discarded lovers
whose letters you read under the covers,

the mere glimpse of whom sets your heart athrob,
with memories of nights that will threaten to rob
you of your much-needed sleep.
So please when you want to weep about the past,
just bloody well make this latest lover last.

PALE EMBERS
COULD
EXPLODE
INTO WILD
WILDFIRE

Journey of the Souls

This poem was inspired by the book, *Journey of Souls, Case Studies of Life between Lives*, by Michael Newton, which affirms that our existence is not limited to the boundaries of our physical beings. I received the book from a dear friend, who went to great lengths to ensure that he could present it to me in person. He died two months later. When I read the book following his passing, I realized why he had been so determined to give it to me.

If you find yourself apart
from the one who holds
the key to your heart,
your sense of desolation
may find consolation
if you know that certain souls,
destined to live, learn and grow together,
will never truly part,
for they will forever remain a part of each other,
whether in this life or in another

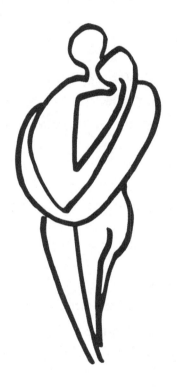

How Do I Love You?

Have you ever thought how absurd
it is that in English we have only one word
to describe how you love your fiancé, the songs of Beyonce,
blueberry pancakes or mocha chocolate ice cream shakes.

Clearly we don't feel exactly the same
about them so we need another name
to reveal how we revere our wife, our lover or our mother,
as opposed to a mountain hike, a grilled cheese sandwich
or a brand new electric bike.

Ancient Greeks solved the problem with a love words list.
Six varieties are known to exist.
The first is Philia, describing how we care about
a comrade, a sister or our brother.
While Eros is the passion you feel for a very special other.
(It's a wild, uncontrolled love that will drive you mad,
before, during and after an addictive relationship goes bad.)

Agape is universal, selfless love we share with each other,
full of empathy and compassion as we look after one another.

During this time of social distancing we need more Ludus,
insisting on playful fun rather than resisting laughing, flirting, light

romancing or even a night of tango dancing.
A game changer would be to practice Philautia--love of self,
e.g. never having to explain, blame, forget or lose oneself.

You could commit to Pragma, a brave endeavor,
committing to a relationship meant to last forever.
Not falling head over heels,
but standing in love reveals how it feels,
when, even though you are mad at your husband or your wife
you cleave together. You don't pack up and leave your life.

We can learn lots about love from those old Greek sages,
whose wisdom has lasted over the ages.

Like avoid too much Eros if you don't want a broken heart
(which is most likely when you and your crazy lover part.)

Instead, cultivate Philia with a trustworthy friend,
knowing that this deep connection need never end.

Then enjoy Ludus, dinner and a late night dance,
without feeling the need for crazy romance.

Work with your Pragma partner to release
feelings that don't increase
a sense of deep and lasting peace.

Most important of all,

learn to love YOU and to your own Self be true.

Then spread Agape wherever you go

because as the Greeks knew and now you know

our world will be in a far better place,

if you and I and all of us create

a more peaceful, joyous and loving space.

. PRAGMA, .   . US, AGA,

.JS, LUDUS, AGAP(,   . IA, PRAGMA, Ph

DUS, AGAP(, PHiLAUTiA, PRAGMA, PHiLiA, ERO>

AGAP(, PHiLAUTiA, PRAGMA, PHiLiA, EROS, LUDU>

'HiLAUTiA, PRAGMA, PHiLiA, EROS, LUDUS, AGAP

. PRAGMA, PHiLiA, EROS, LUDUS, AGAP(, PHiJ

'iLiA, EROS, LUDUS, AGAP(, PHiLAUTiA, PP

'.UDUS, AGAP(, PHiLAUTiA, PRAGMA,

'P(, PHiLAUTiA, PRAGMA, PHiJ'

'UTiA, PRAGMA PHiLiA, '

'-MA, PHiLiA, ER^

'A, EROS. '

'J:'

40

Your Turn

Use this space to draw what you desire.

CHAPTER 3

Becoming Me

My life has been an endless quest to know myself. I try to achieve my potential and lead the most purposeful satisfying and positive existence I can possibly manage. It's about findin my "bliss," as Joseph Campbell describes the sense of peace when we know we're on track. When you know who you are and what you are really meant to do, don't let anyone derail you by telling you what you should think, feel or do. You are the captain of your ship. You hold the compass.

But staying true to yourself, especially during a time of chaos and confusion, is the hardest thing in the world. There are so many voices trying to make themselves heard, fingers pointin every which way. It is then that you have to listen to your inn voice, to hear the wisdom of your higher self, your intuition, inner guide, call it what you will. Let it show you the way. Listen. The voice inside you will tell you the truth - *your* trutl Learn to rely on your inner guidance, whether it's to help you create a master plan for your life, or simply to get you throug the next few minutes, days or weeks.

Apply your inner wisdom as you move in the direction of that which lifts and energizes you, away from people or activities which drain your energy and take you down. Follov your dream, no matter what anyone else says. When you and your soul are headed in the same direction the most incredible things happen. Even before the world begins to fin balance again, be open to the magical, the mystical and the inexplicable. There is an old saying, "when the student is ready, the teacher appears." When you are truly committed, as you need things, ideas, people, will turn up, at exactly the right moment in time.

Set your sights on your own star, keep your compass at hand, and bravely follow the destiny you choose to create. Remember that "this too shall pass."

Grace

Sometimes we allow ourselves to be defined by labels attached to us in childhood, whether by well-meaning elders or unkind peers. Unless you are happy with them, ignore them. We are limitless. Unbounded. Infinite in our possibilities. And by the way, I am not clumsy. I just pretend to be to make people feel better around me. (Not true.)

As a child
they called me Grace
to make light of a real disgrace,
for I was clumsy beyond belief
although I turned my dilemma into light relief.

Giggling and laughing,
I crashed into walls and tripped over air,
but always bounced back with nary a care.
Slipping and sliding I raced at a reckless pace
seemingly unaware of time, place or space.

One day I fell so hard I could not rise.
With no way to stand up that I could devise,
unable to will the power to get up and go
I finally had to let go.
Alone and desperate, sick of the race
I learned the true meaning of Grace.

Now on a new journey as a more peaceful me,
I strive to be more full of Grace,
Though still rarely ever grace-ful.

I Am Woman

Many years ago, during a very difficult time, a dear friend helped me create this mantra for me to repeat. I said the words hundreds of times, often with tears streaming down my face. I still repeat it out loud because I need to remind myself of who I am.

I am beautiful.

I am radiant.

I am loved.

I am woman.

I am peaceful.

I am powerful,

I am prosperous.

I am strong.

I am capable.

I am in ~~control~~ the flow*

* I changed "in control" to " in the flow" when it became clear that I am in control of absolutely nothing, except how I react to people, situations and things I can't control.

46

What would your mantra say?

I am calm
I am steady
I am strong
And I bend

I go with the flow
when the spirit leads me
I stay the course
when I want to spin out

When I write songs
And sing
my love has a vessel
to grow

Red Lady

I travelled thousands of miles to Africa where I first lost, then found, then ultimately became true to myself, but I have discovered that there is an unexplored continent within each of us waiting to be discovered, a place of joy and sorrow, of darkness and light, with limitless potential, challenging every aspect of our being. To respond to its call is to be forever transformed, for it is during this safari of a soul that we confront who we are and who we can become.

A thousand years ago or more,
I drew a red lady ready to soar.
Arms outstretched, naked and free,
uncontained and unrestrained,
she was the me I always wanted to be.

But fearful and tearful,
masked and disguised,
I was a hollow shell in a self-imposed hell.
I realized that to become that me
I would have to find a new way to be.

I stopped crying and started relying
on my inner truth to show me the way.
But it was ancient wisdom, though just as true now
that taught me how to release the bonds

I had created to hold me tight,
and discard the barriers
I had erected to keep out the light.

"Know thyself," intoned the Oracle of Delphi,
"to thine own self be true if you ever want to fly."
So, please release yourself from impossible demands
and begin creating your own new plans.

A thousand years ago or more
I embarked from a safe and familiar shore
and willed myself to soar.
Arms outstretched, naked and free,
unconstrained and unrestrained.
No more fears
and no more tears,
able to be forevermore ME.

A Box Called Me

This poem was inspired by an exercise in which you draw a square with nine smaller boxes inside, each labeled with wha occupies your life. In an ideal world, the boxes should incluc friends, job, children and community activities, as well as tir for ourselves.

When I drew my box,
It seemed that the square
meant for me was filled with air.
There were plenty of boxes for family and friends,
serving the poor, my job and more,
but mine was like an empty drawer.

It seemed the others had grown and migrated,
while my square had shrunk and dissipated.
The box called me had ceased to be.
It's time, I declared,
that this situation is repaired.
I must show that I care not just about we
but I also care about me.

It's hard to get out of a cage at any age,
but when we make a belated effort to locate,
then deflate the outdated, antiquated expectations
that cause palpitations because they have expanded

beyond the normal boundaries that should surround us,
escaping may seem beyond belief,
so let me give you cause for relief.

For my part, I promise to make a brand new start.
I will try not to solve another person's problem
like the author of a Dear Abby column.
I will learn a new way of seeing and being,
and how to embrace another
without turning into his or her mother.
I will get off my treadmill,
and learn to sit still, just chill,
allow goodwill to flow in as well as out.
I may soon doubt this solution
but if I make a firm resolution
there could be a revolution,
or at least an evolution in the space called me.
Perhaps a redistribution of the squares would help,
a substitution in one or two
instead of what others might view as a dangerous coup.

Dammit, it's time to open the door. Now watch me soar!
I'll start to write, take up kickboxing and learn to fight.
Practice yoga, then meditate with all my might.
Free my mind and remind myself
that from this moment forward I'll start anew,
say adieu to strife in my life.

Oh dear, I can see the look on your face.
Please don't worry, I won't displace you,
my child or my brother.
I would never abandon a friend or my mother.
I'll stick to my job, my service to others,
only release what leaves me feeling diminished,
and work to complete the me that's unfinished.

Okay. I guess your reaction
means another plan of action.
I'll forget my crazy dreams.
Besides, all the squares are full again.
I will put my bold campaign on hold
until one day, I pray, before I'm too old,
I'll find a way to claim my space,
a place to be in and out of a box called Me.

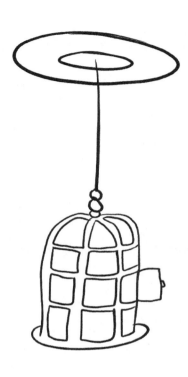

Playing Hooky

Do you ever wake up and say,
sorry, but I'm not coming in to life today,
In fact I'm going to walk, okay, run away,
find a safe space, a quiet place
to disappear, not for months or for years.

Just for now while I release my fears
about all that is happening (or not) to me.
I need time to be,
to hide from the endless tide of bad news
and continuous dread and remind myself
of what Bob Marley once said,
that "everything's gonna be all alright,"
and that I can deal with what lurks in the night,
when worries keep me tossing, turning,
seemingly never ever learning
that "this too shall pass"
and that "bless and release"
is the key to inner peace.

I must know that my glass is "half full,"
not the other way around,
And that I SHALL REBOUND.
It will relieve my fears

If I believe that I have the courage
to change the things I can
and accept without being discouraged
what I cannot control,
and the wisdom to know my role.

I should never make the inference that
blockages are a hindrance,
but instead remember that persistence
may be the way to win the day.
Recall Winston Churchill's intonation
as he spoke to the people of his troubled nation:
"Never give in. Never give in,
never, never, never, never ... "

So if you are ready to moan
about your inability to find stability,
know that there are several ways to go:
persistence, resistance or a new concept: FLOW.
Best achieved by heading back to bed
to clear your head while you repeat,
"Nothing will defeat me."
Convinced that you are invincible,
Pull up the covers and become invisible.

Nothing Will
Defeat Me.

The life of my choice

How can you work toward creating the life of your choice?

Practice everyday
Guitar lessons, vocal lessons,
horse lessons, schedule, a couple
a day. Get to 3 hours! Solid!
Less drinking. Stay the 'course.'
Good diet, exercise, be present,
enjoy life, loosen up,

If you are there already, how can you help someone else get there, too?

Remember what I have
achieved + help when the
opportunity arises.

FREE SPACE TO DOODLE, PLAY AND BE!

Free at Last

It took decades, but I finally followed the message of the Oracle of Delphi to "Know thyself." As I began to know and become true to myself, it became easier to tap into the never-ending source of love, power and energy that I believe connects and empowers us all.

Love, power and energy.
Words that express all I want to be.
Fueling my body, my mind and soul,
creating in me a brand new goal.
To power the world with my energy
Sparking love and hope for all to see,
knowing my destiny is to be
courageously, outrageously, joyously free
by finally being completely me.

If Only

If only I had more money ... if only I had the right relationship
If only my kids stopped fighting ... if only COVID-19 had
never happened. If only the world wasn't upside down. If only
climate change wasn't ruining our lives ... I would be happy.
Sound familiar? I spent years believing that true happiness lay
outside myself. Buried under the chaos and confusion of my
daily life, I yearned for a respite from all that was happening. I
ached for peace and the possibility of joy.

It took a total breakdown of all I had ever known and believed
for me to discover that the essence of happiness comes not
from what happens outside me, but how I am inside. It was an
earth-shattering revelation, for I can no longer blame events,
people, my upbringing or even the coronavirus for my lack of
inner peace.

Think about the people you know who seem happy. Chances
are they aren't the ones with the perfect anything in their lives
except maybe their attitudes. However these rare individuals
have moved from being controlled by external events and
influence to be able to remain calm, centered and in balance,
no matter what happens.

Bad things happen, to us and to those we love. But despite all
the things that rip into our lives, we have a choice - to lash ou
or become self-destructive and hurt ourselves - or roll with th
punches and go with the flow, knowing that everything that
happens is part of our growth. You don't have to be a guru or

a saint to achieve inner peace. You do have to work at it though.

Accepting life as it comes, and trusting that we're okay, no matter what, demands learning to control our thoughts so they don't run away with us. Wise teachers talk about living in the present, neither regretting the past, nor anticipating the future. One way to do that is to follow a spiritual discipline to help you find your center and stay there. I'm terrible at staying still for any length of time, but during the past few months I have tried to sit quietly and meditate, or just listen to music or draw.

It doesn't matter what you do as long as your mind and spirit have a chance to be alone with each other. It's in that union that you experience real peace and true joy. Despite the uncertainty that surrounds you, choose to maintain harmony in your life as you take full responsibility for who you are and what you wish to contribute to our world. Radiate peace and joy wherever you go, knowing that what you give to others is what you will receive. These are difficult times during which to stay positive, but we will get through them, just as our ancestors managed to find their way through other challenging periods. We have to "keep calm and carry on," as we work to manifest a vision of a fair, sustainable future for all.

CHAPTER 4

Tinkering with Life, Toying with Death

Millions around the world are grappling with the loss of a loved one due to the pandemic. Awakening every morning with a gaping hole in their hearts, they wonder whether they ever will be happy again. Knowing that life is precious and ephemeral reminds us to be aware of the gift that each day offers to us; another chance to love more, give more and express how we feel to those we love before it's too late.

After Dan was killed, Amy lived below me in a condo in West Hollywood. When she was upset with me (which happened quite often in those days) she would stomp down the steps, slam the door, then crack it open while shouting, "I LOVE YOU!" This broke the ice, made me smile and usually sorted out the problem, for we both knew that any moment could be our last and we didn't want the final words between us to be unkind.

Those early years were extremely hard for both of us. It was only by transforming the pain of Dan's loss into a force for good that we were able to go beyond merely surviving and find ways to feel joyous again. It helped that I felt Dan's presence around me as a mischievous spirit who knew what I was up to and wanted to help. I was uncertain whether I should tell others about my belief in my ability to communicate with those no longer physically present, but I have learned that my

62

experiences with my unseen guides and mentors mirror those of countless others who, like me, often felt too embarrassed to share them.

A few months after Dan's death, Amy and I discovered an electric typewriter that held within its memory his college essays. When we turned the machine on, it began typing a story about how Dan had run into the poet Ralph Waldo Emerson (then a sprightly 185 years of age) in a seedy bar in South Central Los Angeles. Dan described in detail his leather jacket, with the words, "The Great American Scholar," written on the back, and how Ralph took them on a wild motorcycle ride to the stacks in the UCLA.

Seeing the students, barely awake over their books, Ralph laboriously crawled onto a table where he harangued them about the importance of learning. As they began to sit up and listen, he boomed, "The one thing in the world, of value, is the active soul. This every man is entitled to; this every man contains within him, although, in almost all men, obstructed, and as yet unborn." (You'll have to read the rest of Dan's story* to learn what happened next ...)

As Dan's words appeared on the paper, as though typed by invisible hands, the concept of the "active soul" awakened something deep inside me. I wanted my spirit to be fully activated, unobstructed and reborn, able to fulfill my highest potential, both for myself and for our world.

It's a wish I would have for each one of you—an idea that I hope will fuel you during these challenging times. As you allow yourself to be true to yourself, you will inspire those around you to activate their souls and begin to live fully, love much and leave the world a better place.

" What is success? To laugh often and much; to win the respect of intelligent people and the affection of children....to appreciate the beauty; to find the best in others; to leave the world a bit better, whether by a healthy child, a garden patch... to know even one life has breathed easier because you have lived. This is to have succeeded! "

- Ralph Waldo Emerson

*To read the rest of Dan's story about Ralph Waldo Emerson, please visit kathyeldon.com.

Wild and Precious

What do you want to do with your wild and precious life? (Read Mary Oliver's poem, "The Summer Day" to get you started.)

Playing with DNA

CRISPR is a technology that can be used to edit genes. Scientists use CRISPR to find a specific bit of DNA inside a cell and alter it. In October of 2020, two women scientists wo the Nobel Chemistry Award for their research on CRISPR, a technology that will change our world.

Now that we can play with DNA,
edit genomes that display
possible cataracts, anemia or cystic fibrosis,
is it possible to cut out neurosis,
narcissism, bulimia or psychosis?
Eliminate strands that might lead to racism
or anything else that could create a schism
between religions, cultures and more.
DNA that could result in war.
Remove pigmentation from our genetic code,
café au lait could be the new mode.
One color for all means no discrimination
among people in a diverse nation.

CRISPR out sequences that might make us cruel,
bashing others because we hate a rule,
like wearing a mask when it's clear that it's wise,
and not doing so could lead to the early demise
of someone who deserves another sunrise.

Apply those molecular scissors
to create more artists, writers and singers,
dancers, lovers and all types of givers.
Use tech tools to stop potential fools
from destroying democracy through their hypocrisy.

Someone please design a new template for humankind.
a kind human who is color-blind
but sees with clear vision a world without division.

Sadly, altering DNA can't solve our situation
and we can't wait for the next generation.
It is up to us for the re-creation
of how we want to be.
So, if it's not you and me - now,
then who will it be, when and how?

Six months to live

If you knew you had six months to live, what would you do?

Where Do We Go When We Die?

This is an homage to the *Dead Parrot Sketch*. If you don't know Monty Python then you aren't really alive.

Where do we go when we die?

Do we graduate life and fly,

tassels twirling in the sky?

Do we soar in blinding light

or lie in unending night

contemplating each mortal sin

with nary a heavenly violin.

How will we be when we pass away?

Will we yearn a return to earthly fray?

Or eager to make ethereal hay?

I'd like think that all of us

quickly shed the annoying fuss.

Liberated at last from human pain,

no more hurt, no more blame

Uncontained and unrestrained,

sans demeanor we once maintained,

now doing as we please,

no more waiting till another agrees.

Seeking the spirits we loved and lost,

ignoring those we blithely tossed,

we unite with souls once adored,
hearts as one, our love restored.

What happens after we are extinct,
when we have ceased to be?
Here is what I'd like to think.
When I am bereft of life
and have left behind all earthly strife
my spirit will be a noisy one,
demanding others join the fun.
For I am planning a forever vacation,
a rest first, then re-creation?

unfurling
wings

"There is no ending, no beginning, only the infinite passion of life."
- Federico Fellini

Blink

A reminder to live fully, love much, and leave the world a better place because you were in it. Then you can soar smiling ...

When you're young you never think
that life could be over in a blink.
But then your mileage gauge ticks faster,
leading you to the ultimate disaster.
When days, months and even years
fly by filled with joy and tears,
You realize your mortality
and that one day
you too will be a fatality.
But instead of being fearful,
I choose to remain relentlessly cheerful.
I plan to die from too much giggling.
Wriggling with delight in the fading light,
blissfully unaware of my plight,
I will slip gently into eternal night.

After my son Dan was killed at the age of 22, I was determined to live as fully as possible. However, over the years, I forgot and took life for granted. The pandemic reminds us of the imminent possibility of grave illness or death - and should heighten our awareness of the importance of living fully and loving as much as possible. This is a time to celebrate those we love and remind them of how much we care about them. If not now, when? Connect now.

Phantom Limb

In this poem I tried to remember how I felt one year after my son Dan's death.

I don't have words to explain the grief I feel,
the look in my eyes should be enough to reveal
the ache in my heart and how close I am to falling apart.
It has been a year but as with a phantom limb that hurts
although it is not there I remain in indescribable pain.

Since Dan passed, 365 days have passed.
There is a belief that by now I should have found some relief.
But if asked I would say that my grief will not go away.
I want to be wrong, but right now I would happily die
if it meant I would never again cry for he
whom I loved beyond measure.

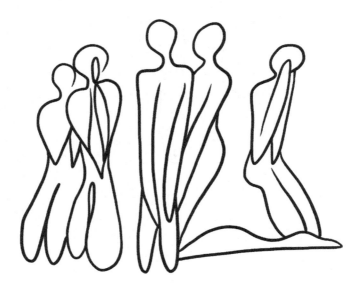

The memory of the one whom I so treasured
lies buried in my heart though his soul has long departed.
Hawk-free, wheeling sky high, he has learned to fly,
dipping, diving, riding currents of air up there, somewhere.
Not fair I say, for his spirit to so freely play
while mine remains earthbound
planted on hard and unyielding ground.

When, I ask, can my soul join his?
Free of the need to be a solid me,
while he, ephemeral, ethereal, invisible
can with childlike joy and infinite grace
eternally soar across time and space.

When I finally ascend I intend to transcend
all that has been holding me down,
Shedding trappings I shall head toward the sky,
determined to fly just as high.
Spirit soaring, pain released
I shall finally find true peace.

Finding Wings to Fly

For my daughter Amy, who has always encouraged me to stop flapping, have faith and soar.

Dearest Amy Louise,

I promise you that I will not undo this demand,
so please consider it a loving command.
When I am unwell and past my sell by date,
I would hate for you to try to hold on to me,
for I wish to go with grace and dignity.
So may I enlist you to assist
when it's time for me to cease to exist?

Don't resist, my beloved daughter,
for you are not leading me to the slaughter,
but only fulfilling my request to do
what I believe is best for me and for you.
You see, I never want to forget your name,
or do anything that would make you feel ashamed.

So this is how I would like to depart.
First we will sip some Yorkshire Gold tea,
with honey for you, but none for me,
Next please take me for an airplane ride,

dipping and diving in a clear blue sky,
Then when it's time, not before,
fling open the airplane door,
now push me out and watch me soar.

You know how long I have flapped,
when I really wanted to fly.
So please do not cry as I take flight
heading towards a brilliant light.
Don't be sad, my darling Amy.
Be glad that I am finally free,
and that we shall be reunited
Throughout all eternity.

Noisy Spirits

Twenty years ago or more,
my son Dan departed for some distant shore.
But I don't believe that any more,
for if he has gone that far, how is it
that I feel him around me almost every day,
smiling in his inimitable way
(mostly in the half light of approaching night,
then gone if I look too closely.)

I sometimes see him in my dreams.
It seems he appears when
I'm most anxious and concerned.
Then he stands above me looking down
with a tiny frown as though to say,
remember I'm never far away,
and one way or another as Bob Marley always said,
everything's gonna be alright.
Things will look better in the morning light.

Other times I feel him on my shoulder,
encouraging me to speak up, be bolder.
He says that I must not doubt his existence
for there is no distance between us.
I must ask for assistance, though,

for after all, spirits aren't meant
to appear to interfere.

So Dan, I'm asking you now how we can
heal our ailing planet because dammit,
we didn't plan it to turn out this way.
I know, I know what you'll say,
we're beyond remiss in what we've done,
but don't dismiss this plea,
for we urgently need help
to ignite the change we wish to see,
the one Gandhi said we each have to be.

So Dan, can you please bring your man
Mahatma to an emergency meeting?
I'll organize the seating.
Hey, while you're inviting,
could you set up an RBG sighting?
Let's include Martin Luther King,
Bobby Kennedy and his brother,
my father and my mother,
and any others who can be of service
because I'm super nervous
that we have left this all too late,

I hate to think that our world could be finished,
our seas polluted, our crops diminished
because we haven't heeded
the wise beings who preceded us,
Like Chief Seattle who was said to declare
that air shares its spirit with all the life it supports.

That day he went on to exhort in his powerful way
that the earth does not belong to man.
Who then? I say.
Man belongs to the earth, he said.
And all things are connected.
It's a concept we have long rejected.

So now can we recall Chief Seattle's words
and act to forestall the doom and gloom that lie ahead?
Just imagine. If we unite to fight planetary blight,
we can start to set things right - head towards the light.
Connected to one another, to Spirit and to our land,
we can create a bright new future for humankind.
Instead of grief, pain and sorrow,
we can ensure a kind, loving and equitable tomorrow.

Where do you think we go when we die?

CHAPTER 5

A Better Tomorrow

Now is the time to do all you can to maintain harmony in your life and take full responsibility for who you are and what you wish to contribute to our troubled world.

Radiate peace and joy wherever you go, knowing that what you give to others is what you will receive. These are difficult times during which to stay positive, but we will get through them, just as our ancestors managed to find their way through challenging periods. We have to "keep calm and carry on," as we maintain a vision of a fair, sustainable and kind future for us all.

KEEP
CALM
AND
CARRY
ON

No one is watching

Many of the doodles in this book acted as a form of art therapy when I was going through difficult patches in my life. Allow your subconscious to reveal how you feel about yourself - and the world around you. Go for it.

Get in the Way

I felt fortunate to hear John Lewis speak. With courage, conviction and a wicked sense of humor, he encouraged us all to make mischief.

"Get in the Way,"
John Lewis proclaimed,
"Get in trouble, good trouble," he explained.
That means get out of your bubble,
speak truth to power
and don't let your belief in democracy sour.

Find strength in unity, power in community.
Focus on inequality, injustice and the immorality of
those who stand for rights of the unborn
while turning a blind eye to those they scorn
for being another religion or race,

Bring your brothers and sisters together.
Disturb the status quo wherever you go.
Point to a new destination for this powerful generation.
Believe you can achieve all you have been waiting for
peace, justice and much, much more.

Never give up, never give in,
be courageous in all you do,
channeling the powerful energy
flowing through me and through you.

Watch for the glow of John Lewis's star
beaming light through the darkest night.
Although he may seem far away,
listen inside and you can hear him say,
"Get in the way, cause trouble,
good trouble every day."

For now that John Lewis is gone,
we must be the light, shining bright,
reminding others to stick with the fight.

Believe you can achieve all you have been waiting for.

For One and For All

Article one, section two of the Constitution of the United States declared that any person who was not free would be counted as three-fifths of a free individual for the purposes of determining congressional representation. The "Three-Fifths Clause" thus increased the political power of slaveholding states.

Millions deserve restitution
from the institution that enslaved their kin
when all they craved was the ability
to enjoy the liberty promised in our constitution.
When Jefferson stated that "all men are created equal,"
he really meant only certain people.

Not those who were black,
nor children who were half and half,
fathers betrayed by their offsprings' lightness
and striking likeness to those
who disowned, but owned them.
Jefferson is said to have kept
enslaved four of his children
after writing his finest creation,
the revolutionary proclamation
of freedom for his infant ... nation.

Our founding fathers defamed
future generations when

they insanely claimed that
a slave counted as three-fifths of a man,
though they worked more than any human can.

To heal deep wounds caused by
centuries of misuse and abuse
we must rise and devise
a powerful disruption
of this immoral corruption.

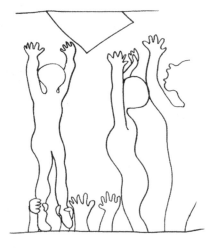

Disband and remand vigilantes,
rifles in hand, who scream "all lives matter"
as they batter those who march,
hearts filled with sorrow,
hoping for a better tomorrow.

For once and for all, stop rampant racism,
fight fear and fascism.
Do all you can to unite the equal people of our land —
for one and for all.

Purple Heart

Soldiers earn a Purple Heart when they are wounded in
service. Just think about how great it would be not to have to
sacrifice anything but intolerance, bigotry and hypocrisy to
turn our hearts a lovely shade of purple.

Imagine how our country could be

if we focused on the needs of WE,

not just me, me, me, me.

Instead of being cruel or mean,

let's hold others in full esteem,

and team together to build a collective dream.

We all want this country to flourish and to grow,

so treat strangers as our sisters and our brothers,

and seniors as our fathers and our mothers.

Create success for one another

instead of suppressing or oppressing each other.

Be the solution to toxic pollution

caused by being lewd, crude or rude.

For if humankind is truly kind

we can heal our divided nation.

So here's an idea of my creation.

Invite your family to a reunion

Then watch for those scared of real union,
standing apart shielding their hearts
behind armor of red or blue.
Instead of adding more armament
by picking an angry argument,
use love to melt divisive colors
into a more harmonious hue.

To save the future of the next generation,
let's create a purple-hearted population,
a united nation with no exploitation or condemnation
of red or blue, black or white, me or you.

We can heal
our divided nation

A Sweet Solution

I wrote this on the morning of November 4th, 2020, when our nation was impossibly divided.

Dear Americans, whether red or blue,
now that we are through with the election,
let's find new direction,
release prejudices about each other
and create peace with one another.

Let go of tension. Create a new intention
to unite, not divide,
aware that unity in community
offers opportunity
for new beginnings,
where winning no longer means
one takes all.
That has been our downfall.

We can do better. And here's how.
Call someone who doesn't think the same as you
and talk about a subject where you can agree,
free of emotion or the silly notion
that one of you has to be right
Keep it light!

Discuss the weather, but not climate change, okay?

Keep that one at bay.

Religion? Not so much. Hard to keep a light touch.

Football (mmm ... tough call,

maybe not such a good idea after all.)

How about sweet treats that you both like to eat?

That's a hard subject to beat.

It should be good for a minute or two,

then hang up the phone before you feel the inclination

to indignantly discuss the state of the nation.

Feel a sense of elation

as you create a new foundation

for a relationship that can offer kinship

rather than triggering enmity

that could turn you into enemies.

I know we can do it!

But we have to commit not to split or quit

for we have only one planet, dammit,

and we have a tight deadline.

So instead of maligning one another,

Let's align with each other.

You do your bit, and I'll do mine

and together we will weather this challenging time.

Good Trouble

John Lewis said, "Cause good trouble."
Here's how I can cause good trouble everyday:

In my family.

In my neighborhood.

In my job.

In my community.

One Human Race

There is only one human race. How can I hear and accept others, even though they don't look like me or I don't agree with them? How can I help create a civil society - a better world, not just for people like me, but for all:

In my family.

In my neighborhood.

In my community.

In our world.

Seek Solutions, Not Problems

My son Dan said, "seek solutions, not problems."
What solutions can I seek to help solve issues:

In my family.

In my neighborhood.

In my job.

In my community.

What Can I Do to Help?

Mother Teresa said, "just respond to people's needs." What can I do to respond to the needs of individuals:

In my home.

In my neighborhood.

In my job.

In my community.

In our world.

This is Your Mother Speaking

Do you even see what you're doing to me?
I give you everything and you just take, take, take
without realizing the sacrifices I make.
Unaware of how to care, much less to share.

You ask why my temperature is rising.
Well, it's easy to explain, I'm feeling overheated
and defeated by who and how you are.
This unkind treatment has gone too far.

I am your mother, after all, not some random other.
I am the air. The land. The sea. All are me.
You are the child of this we.
Two of three breaths you take is from the air I make.
I spawned you and all living creatures from my womb
but when I watch you looking at me, I know that I'm doomed.

I see your superficial gaze,
but perhaps your vision is blurred by the haze
of smoke from forests ablaze,
leaving no safe space, no hidden place
from infernos which rage and rage.
You say you love me.
So why do you use and abuse me,

capture my treasures without measure
leak oil, dump chemicals and worse,
Honestly my child, I hate to say it,
but I see you as a curse.

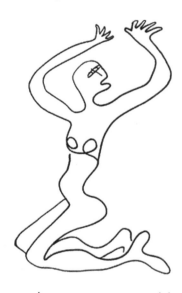

You poison my oceans, bleach coral reefs,
hook, snare, net my innocent creatures deep beneath.
Apparently you feel that somehow I'll be able to recreate
what has taken millenia to procreate.
Clearly this is not working for me, nor for you.
Remember, as I gave you breath,
I shall be responsible for your death.

So stop being reckless with the one you should love.
Give more to me than you receive.
Say no to what you don't need,
sparkly objects born of greed.

Do not be deceived and believe there
are other sources for my precious resources.
When my land is parched and my sky is gray
with ash and soot from the fires that have burned away
all my grasses and flowers, trees and more,
there will be worse pain for you in store.

For my sea too will be free of life
save formless shapes in the deep recesses
of my hidden crevices,
ready to make a quiet entrance,
millenia from now.

New life begun in my deep womb
will emerge again to dispel earth's gloom.
Swim first with newly webbed feet,
then walk on land, a remarkable feat.
From then we know that wings will grow.
And in the clear blue skies of tomorrow,
I will finally forget my sorrow.

Seeing creatures live in peace and safely grow
will quell my pain I know.
but if they, like you, descend into greed,
use more than they need,
then they too will have to go.
So please, heed my warning,

and awaken all to a brand new morning,
sparked by mourning for what you have lost.
Treat me as your loving mother
and let's work with each other.
We, the land, the sea, you and me entwined,
together can save all humankind.
Hurry please, for you must appreciate
that very soon it will be too late,
as you, my child, are past your sell-by date.

I am the Air.
the Land.
the Sea.
All are Me.

A New Creation

Five months into the Covid shutdown, I awakened in the middle of the night with this poem flowing through me. It was the first- and perhaps one of the most important messages of all those I have transmitted from my Noisy Spirits.

Imagine a nation,
a new creation
united in peace and love

Imagine a nation,
our creation,
disruption dispelling corruption,
igniting positive change

Imagine the world as this nation.
Community powering unity
over time and space.
Imagine this unity
sparking opportunity
across generations and race

Imagine this nation,

a new creation

bringing joy and grace

Imagine this nation.

Imagine it now.

Our creation.

Our nation.

So what's your part - and how?

> # Unity sparking opportunity across generations and race

Creating a New Vision

What are your dreams for the future?

Hope Rising: A Final Musing

A global pandemic swept away the illusion of security in our lives. The effects of racism and social injustice roiled our cities, and the impact of climate change forced us to ask existential questions about our future. But, despite all the difficult times we have endured, we have seen how the human spirit, though beaten down, shattered and battered, has endeavored to rise, to find new hope, to grow and expand, learn to dance again and one day, even to fly.

As we rise from the ashes of our shattered dreams to create a new vision for the future, we can and will find the resilience and strength to manifest them into a new reality. We have an extraordinary opportunity to transform ourselves and our world for the better, but it will require us to work together. Connected and committed to one another, we can transform our collective pain into a powerful, positive force for good.   If we don't, there is no hope, only the acrid smell of smoke in the air.

I know we can do it.

Kathy Eldon

Afterword

By Kathy's Noisy Spirits

I wanted to ask someone famous to wrap up this book, but when I reached out to my Noisy Spirts, it seemed they wante to have the last word. I was delighted when former Secretary General U Thant organized a roundtable to discuss what the should say and invited me to join them. Please note that I di my best to take down everyone's comments, but it was a bit hectic with all those flapping wings and clanking halos.

The Secretary General tapped on a glass to get everyone's attention. "The war we have to wage today has only one goal and that is to make the world safe for diversity," he stated.

Chief Seattle took a long puff on his pipe. Plumes of smoke swirled around him as he began to speak. "All things are bound together. All things connect. All things share the sam breath - the beast, the tree, the man ... the air shares its spiri with all the life it supports. Man does not weave this web of life. He is merely a strand of it. Whatever he does to the web, he does to himself."

When he had finished everyone sat quietly for a moment. President Kennedy broke the silence, saying that he agreed with the Chief, but wondered what people, once they connected with each other, should do to ensure that the planet would survive. "Things do not happen, they are made to happen," he declared.

Suddenly all hell broke loose (which I thought was quite

inappropriate given where we were). It seemed that everyone had a different idea about how to approach the challenges we face. It got really noisy until my son Dan, dove into the conversation. "Seek solutions, not problems," he shouted over the din.

You could hear a pin drop. I was proud when Ruth Bader Ginsberg flashed a smile at Dan, then drew herself to her full height of 5'1", "You can disagree without being disagreeable," she said, glaring over her glasses. "Fight for the things that you care about but do it in a way that will lead others to join you."

Mahatma Gandhi explained what he thought was important. "A nation's culture lies in the hearts and souls of its people," he said. His words struck a chord as the spirits literally rose from their chairs. Ralph Waldo Emerson, wearing his Great American Scholar leather jacket, climbed onto the table before crying out, "The one thing in the world of value is the active soul, free, sovereign, unencumbered ... this every man holds within, but in most it's obstructed and as yet unborn."

There were loud cheers from the crowd. I raised my hand, but no one took any notice. The Secretary General had to shush everyone before I could speak. "I love the idea of an activated soul," I said, "but once souls are awakened, or 'woke,' as we say these days, what should they do?"

Mother Teresa raised her hand. "Just respond to people's needs," she said, her voice sounding surprisingly strong for such a tiny person. Then I remembered what Bishop

Desmond Tutu, surely an angel with skin, once said, "Do a little bit of good wherever you are; it's those bits of good that will overwhelm the planet."

Suddenly, Teddy Roosevelt sprang to his feet, "Do what you can with what you have where you are!" he shouted, slashing the air with his sword. Giving him a look, Eleanor Roosevelt rose and declared, in her dignified way, "You must do the thing you think you cannot do."

Very inspiring, I thought, but there is SO much we have to do to sort out our world. Sir Winston Churchill must have noticed my anxiety. Blowing cigar smoke my way, he launched into a tirade, "Bloody well keep calm and carry on, woman. Every day you may make progress. Yet there will stretch out before you an ever-lengthening, ever-ascending, ever-improving path. You know you will never get to the end of the journey. But this, so far from discouraging, only adds to the joy and glory of the climb."

"It always seems impossible until it's done," Nelson Mandela said reassuringly. Then someone pulled out a harp and another, a harmonica. Soon everyone was clapping and singing. I loved that Nelson Mandela invited Mother Teresa and RBG to join him in an impromptu conga dance.

Dan stood with me as they twirled around the room. "Thanks for listening, Mum," he said, his eyes sparkling. "We've waited a long time to get through to you and all the other earth people who have been screwing up the planet. You can restore balance again, but you have to get cracking. There's very little time left. You'll have to be very creative and work fast."

My eyes welled as I realized that it was time for me to leave. "Always remember that I love you," Dan said, hugging me so tightly I could barely breathe.

Seeing the tears streaming down my face, Maya Angelou enveloped us both in her arms. "Love recognizes no barriers," she whispered, "It jumps hurdles, leaps fences, penetrates walls to arrive at its destination full of hope."

Hope. That word again. Dan smiled as he shook his head. "Remember, Miss Angelou, the *Journey* is the Destination" Reluctantly, I said goodbye to them and tiptoed out of the room. Stepping into the night, I was surprised to hear Martin Luther King call after me, "Only in the darkness can you see the stars."

I looked up. To my surprise, Bob Marley was hovering before me. "Everything's gonna be alright!" He said with a cheeky grin. I held open the door for him as he swooped down to join the noisy flutter of spirits inside.

Everything's Gonna Be Alright

Get Involved

To learn more about Kathy Eldon's belief in the power of individuals to transform themselves and the world around them, please visit kathyeldon.com

To join the *Hope Rising* initiative, or purchase bulk copies of the book, please visit hoperisingproject.com

Creative Visions is a United Nations Non-Governmental organization and social enterprise that Kathy and her daughter Amy founded in 1998 to celebrate the life of artist and photographer, Dan Eldon. Since then, Creative Visions has touched the lives of more than 100 million people through projects and productions incubated or produced by the organization. To get involved, please visit creativevisions.org

To learn more about Dan Eldon's life and legacy and purchase fine art prints of his journal pages, please visit daneldon.org

Some other books by Kathy Eldon

In the Heart of Life
Angel Catcher
Soul Catcher
Love Catcher
Tastes of Kenya
Safari Diary
Making Music in Kenya

Acknowledgments

With gratitude to Michael Bedner, Amy Eldon Turteltaub, Eva Haller, Pat Chandler, Alicia Dougherty and the Creative Visions team for encouraging me to keep channeling my Noisy Spirits. Thank you to Klaus Obermeyer for inspiring, "This is Your Mother Speaking." Special thanks to my multi-talented Creative Designer, Kyle Hollingsworth, Editor, Nicole Melillo and Publisher, Bill Gladstone, who made it possible to get my Noisy Spirits' message out to the world.

Your Turn.

Made in the USA
Las Vegas, NV
16 February 2021

17930304R00069